Your Rightful Childhood:

New and Selected Poems,
1970-1995

Books By Paula Rankin:

By the Wreckmaster's Cottage (1977)
Augers (1981)
To the House Ghost (1985)
Divorce: A Romance (1990)
Your Rightful Childhood: New and Selected Poems (1997)

Your
Rightful
Childhood:
New and Selected Poems,
1970-1995

Paula Rankin

Carnegie Mellon University Press
Pittsburgh 1997

ACKNOWLEDGMENTS:

Many of these poems first appeared in the following
publications:

*Agni Review, American Poetry Review, Arkansas River Review,
Ascent, Back Door, Carolina Quarterly, Chowder Review, Crazy Horse,
Epos, Georgia Review, Kalliope, Laurel Review, Louisville Review,
Memphis State Review, Missouri State Review, The Nation, New
Jersey Review, New Orleans Review, North American Review, Ohio
Review, Partisan Review, Plain Song, Ploughshare, Poem, Poetry
Miscellany, Poetry Northwest, Quarterly West, raccoon, Seneca
Review, Shenandoah, Southern Poetry Review, Tar River Poetry,
Tendril, Three Rivers Poetry Journal, Vanderbilt Review, Westigan
Review, Woman Poet: The South, edited by Dara Wier.*

Publication of this book is supported by a grant from the
Pennsylvania Council on the Arts.

Library of Congress Catalog Card Number 96-83426
ISBN 0-88748-245-7
ISBN 0-88748-246-5

10   9   8   7   6   5   4   3   2   1

CONTENTS

from: *By the Wreckmaster's Cottage*

from: *Augers*

from: *To the House Ghost*

from: *Divorce: A Romance*

Your Rightful Childhood

Three True Stories at the Back

Humbly Submitted to God and My Family

"This quiet Dust was Gentlemen and Ladies, Lads and Girls"
—Emily Dickinson

FROM BY THE WRECKMASTER'S COTTAGE

Poem for Actors

I always wonder what happened
to put them on the far side of the glass,
why they are the channel I watch,
why I am the channel who pays.

I wonder if their mothers rented them
to magazines for models,
if their father knew the president
of something, or if they were simply born
knowing how to walk into a script
and nickname it Life.

I want to know if success
spoiled or redeemed Mary Ann Jones
from life on this side of the screen,
if she still has a nickname she goes by
when using the john like anyone.

I want to plug into their pillows,
to hear what the real dreams say
about rolling so many acts into one,
layers of face we all want to try on
and get paid for, plenty of roles
for an encore, a comeback.

Sideshows

We call them depraved
for what they sell:
Deformity.

We want to say
to the fattest of fat men:
Surely there is something else
you could do
to feed such hunger;
Bearded lady, it would only take a shave.

But then not everyone
can toss fluorescent nipples
and catch them easily as coins
or display the ambiguities of his sex
unabashed. Perhaps these too are callings?

If you have enough quarters,
they will show you everything
you'd only guessed at
from Hermaphrodite's shadow
on the side of the tent
to the glassed-in fetus
of a beast child who,
if he never sees his cut
of suckers' money,
will live as long as a memory
when the canvas drops
and its tenants slip into trucks
leaving the fields full of squashed cups
but no trail

though we go back for days
with more quarters.

Pentecosts

We're told the Apostles
on that day
bloomed swirls of fire
like lit junipers
right out of their brains.
Because we cannot imagine a man,
much less twelve, on fire
and happy about it,
we take this story with a grain of salt
which under microscope would show up
as many grains of envy.

Under microscope envy would be
broken down into tiny mirrors
that reflect us, rubbing sticks
to spark any number of flames,
using our heads like match-ends
to strike dialogues between ourselves
and all we cannot reach by word of mouth—
the dog warming his bones in the sun,
the cricket with so much to say
and no one to translate,
the sounds of trees growing at night,
and each other: the unspoken under microscope
looping the body's limbs to the brain,
a constant simmering brushfire
that keeps us going
as long as there's something to burn.

Under microscope
all the cells want in.
They all want to burn
and be happy about it.

Women Partly Explained

Wind waits for stillness,
a settling down of things.
There is this air that nests
in trees   houses   faces of women
numb with inhaling the unchanging rooms
of their lives. It has something to do
with prime cuts of meat,
with the teeth of husbands and children,
with
      Indians
            tracking
who do not imagine
wood broken down into tables and chairs
who slit open our sleep
like an animal's skin,
their eyes glazed with soft smoke from piñon
where it breaks into prayers for the gods
who mate in the core of the sun,

our dreams the only shelter they have found.

Sacrifices

Starring into the mammoth's fossilized jaw,
I think of all the holes
where we never touch bottom,
cannonballs through civil war soldiers,
gaps left by abominable snowmen
crossing over.

When I touch the spearhead lodged
in his backbone, I remember Indians
gored through their pectoral muscles
with the same weapon, sacrificed to all the gods
who counted: sun, wind, river, rain.
Now here we all come as tourists, pretending
to watch from such distance, planting ourselves
like crops that need no intervention.

Last night I watched a dog
bleed for hours after death,
the god of ignitions satisfied, spinning rubber
towards other intersections

and I found myself asking
whether willingness counts, if the cells
must announce their intention
before they meet tire, razor, bullet,
or a bridge's cement pilings,
if the body must make its leap
with all the pores open

or if getting pushed counts
or even being nudged, lash-blink
by lash-blink, towards the edge
something's always slipping off of.

The Catalog People

Their eyes stay pinned
to something off the page,
as if trying to track their own flesh
drained from sweaters and pants.
A girl in tricot pretends lust
while brassieres deflate
like unfilled orders. The shoes dream
of tracking us into our lives;
furs hoard what little they remember
of beasthood and human blood.

When we slap down their sky
locking them into their sizes
we refuse to imagine their moving
through pages like rooms
swapping tales of our lives.

By the Wreckmaster's Cottage at Assateague

The dunes loosen like winding sheets
and with them all hope
of keeping things covered:
grains at the time, they ride the bay wind
and start over wherever they land.

Slowly the sand releases the boats
to new owners: keel, spar, masthead
jabbed towards sky like the finger of blame.
I run my hand over ribs picked clean
by men who are always arriving first
at scenes of disaster, sifting through bones
for lockets, daguerreotype grins, strands
of hair stripped white by drinking
last thoughts from drowned brains.

I think of passengers huddled in holds
dreaming of impenetrable cypress
like an ark nothing chews through,
of what it must be to go down
in full view of the light
on Assateague Island

like any landlubber,
like those of us who keep falling
through hyphenated light
until sand weaves the coat
that will fit us.

Taking Stew to an Old Woman

She lets me in and I offer the leavings
of yesterday's stew, disguised
in a bright yellow bowl.
I do not know her, know only facts
eyes and ears sponge from a distance:
she is old, alone and nights her porch light
flushes the dark from my bedroom.
I do not tell her of times I have stared
at her half-open slats for eyes
that must, by now, have trained themselves
to ride venetian blinds like a bumpless road
where each traveler lands safely home.

She sets the bowl on a table, explaining
how this room once was the parlor,
how her bed is in the dining room,
how her cupboard creaks less now that she cooks
in the bedroom. Is this what it comes to,
I think, a reconstruction of rooms,
a scrambling of knobs, plates, photographs,
as if the eye might be fooled,
the walls tricked into utter confusion?

Yet nothing seems moved: someone has sprayed
an aerosol can of fine dust. I sit
because she asks me to, because I sense need
like a bottle I found once in the ocean:
the note must have floated for years,
its owner needing me way before then.
I listen to tales of husband and sons
strung out like wash on a clothesline,
limp sleeves almost filling with air.
All the while I am facing her bed,
open as a boat under ceiling.

It has been handed down
through the family, she says
none of whom is present
when an 86-year-old woman
takes out her teeth,

tries hard for her bones
to make some impression
as she slips between sheets
and prays for the dead.

I wonder if I stayed long enough
could I ask my real questions:
how far from me to you?
How to turn loss
into small acts of levitation,
short floats between mattress and ceiling?

I go through the motions of leaving,
my best act, knowing I walk behind her
as I go down the steps. She flicks on
her porch light again

where each night the moths singe their wings
while she rearranges the smallest of rooms,
rescattering the objects of attention
like the rest of us who pray
for the dead and the living.

Hazards: Night Driving on Ice

That night even the ocean stopped
keeping time by tides and froze its collection
of beer cans, shells, bottles stuffed
too late with calls for help.

Then I did not think to ask
whether everyone deludes himself
that he has left in the nick of time?
Perhaps there were others
similarly caught that night
without warning, leaping from barstools,
sofas, beds, into coats, cars, praying
road crews had salted their particular
treads into ice—

but to us they were only
a Buick flipped on its side
a station wagon crunched on a guard rail
lanes packed with the world's worst
skaters, drivers who had no training in skids;

to us they were only wrecks
forecasting shapes we must choose from.
That night the Exxon station
locked its pumps, unplugged its neon flash
like a yanked promise, and we had to ignite
a tank of almost nothing, slide out
on treadless tires
and the blizzard blew into my head,
each microscopic crystal dissolving its
whisper: Now you will learn to be good.

You turned on the radio
and it was snowing there too
all over the songs of true, false,
open, secret, calm, frantic, platonic,
incestuous, right and wrong

Loves, all over each larynx, diaphragm,
nasal twang that swore fidelity
inside the grooves of scratched records.

You thought I was eating my hand.
I was praying
as only the guilt-ridden can
that we were some halfway-fallen angel's
special assignment, that your hands
on the steering wheel, tires spinning
towards home were last chances
for earning wings back.

Long since home,
safely unpacked with one of the stories
of minor disaster that keeps our lives
salvageable, only now do I dare
to look back
for your face
behind the windshield wipers,
your eyes filling/emptying
with blizzard/love

only now do I think to ask
if everyone brings with himself to a window
steamed vision, an inability to wipe stares
clean when aiming them backwards,
salt drifting like snow through the bloodstream,

Lot's wife alive
though hardly well,
hardly breathing.

Taking All We Can With Us

It's always something overlooked,
the monogrammed stick-pin left
on the ledge, the footprint in wet
cement beyond the door where someone
ran screaming, Thief!

Of course we are no more thieves
than anyone who steals
from each unguarded entry
that keeps trying to break into print
as Chapter I of novels we lug through our heads.

Even dust tells a story: it has only two
lives, swirling and landing,
and it lands only on the left-too-long,
the plate never thrown, the chair
never sat in, the face
never twisted in anguish or love.

Moving is our way of confusing the dust,
of convincing ourselves that much
is still unsettled, that we still
have some say in our endings. Sometimes
we even dream there is nothing
we cannot take with us, that we will be first
to perform the real vanishing act.
Even signatures on checks will dissolve
and fly with us for identity.
We will know
and be known
by all we can carry.

There will be nothing to auction or bequest.

On Holding On

All the proof we need,
waiting in our book of picture squares.
Children that were you and I
squared off with popsicles dripping,
baseballs gloved,
skirts hanging, pants bagging,
flipping pages,
holding on—

Pants and skirts stop their sagging
Taking shape on bodies taking
shape.
Swells, bulges, spreads
locked up in flatness
as we in our bursting bodies
were flatly guessing about
how to enter our lives:
smiles of secret knowledge
from passed around books
and wet pants.

Turning slowly now,
We know these faces better;
we search the eyes instead.
Friends, glass-eyed, grinning,
glasses held in toasts,
picnic tables, Christmas trees,
the burlesque of it all
is making us smile,
so that later,
eyes will not matter;

We can say, Here it is!
Look! We were laughing

Now we train the children
that are ours
Look at the man now
Smile at his hand
One two three

Here it is!
Look!
You are smiling
You are happy here with us
Come into the picture book

Reflections in the Eye Specialist's Waiting Room

Here we are,
the people who do not see well.
There is no talk;
I pass the time blurring people's faces.
They are mostly old men.
I am called next;
I have drops put in my eyes.
I ask, will it stop burning?
I am given a tissue,
told to go back and wait.
I think, now would be such a safe
time to cry—
I will bite myself when no one is looking.
Instead, wishing I had worn a calf-length skirt
all the way down the hall where
old men are watching me come back,
I return, sit in a different chair.
I get out a cigarette and a book of matches.
I strike.
It is not until I try to make contact
between the two
that I am afraid:
my eyes cannot find the lighting point.
Between it and the flame is the
Old Woman,
the one I have seen in mirrors,
looking down the road of my face.

I slam my eyes and burn her.

I inhale.

For the Obese

We are always saying,
with will power,
their buttons would slip into holes
over their bellies, their zippers
would close like a mouth
which gets the last word
in the old argument
of why some eat to stay alive
while some eat to summon impossible lovers
who fill every inch of the body.

Then we say it's hard to find their eyes
or the stand their bones take
so far underground.
We lock them into their bodies,
slipping the key into our pocket,
fingering it from time to time
as reminder of those few wars
we aren't a part of.

Where We Are

I think it's the way
you moved through your life:
as if you were no one at all.

I never saw gray become anyone;
on you it was a silver shirt
I watched moving in and out
of the classroom, into your car,
down the right hand side of the road,
straight. Home free by 10:15.

Oh, I am no one too,
but that's another address.
It will still be me calling your name
from the top of the roller coaster,
waiting for the conductor to show up
to ask for my ticket
to throw me off when he discovers
I never bought one.

We come together in the middle of a forest,
not convincing each other
that either method of travel is best;
certain only that we move,
that we meet,
warm hands before a fire,
set out again to clear our small paths
like no one, no one at all.

To the Ox-Cart Driver

Stropping oxen, you nudge through town
with bedsprings, bottles, chimney bricks,
riding the rumor that there are always men
who'll try anything on.

I stare into ox eyes
that scald me with their dumbness,
their blank recognition of road
and burden, their disregard
for the changing directions of wind.

You hold up your collections
of drained sleeves, pants, shoes,
telling me how washing will shrink
them to fit. I do not say

how it is ox I want to barter for,
how I need to try on hide blunt-nosing its way
through the dark without questioning,
until yokes press as lightly on skin
as a shirt passed down
from hand to hand to hand.

The Shell-Gatherer

At Ocracoke, I met a woman
who stayed on long after others
had ferried to mainland winters,
leaving boats and shops slammed
against tourists
and the hungry wind.

She stayed to ferret low tides alone,
when the ocean, cleaning house,
dumps its dustpan of expendables:
dwellings whose tenants have drowned
into new lives as shark cells,
fish eyes, gull feathers.

We combed seaweed,
wondering at the nutritional value of snarls
tossed at our feet by hurricane
and tidal wave. She chose only whole shells,
cupping oceans to her ear
like Anglo-Saxon riddles,
nicknaming each conch and Scotch-bonnet,
explaining drained lives,
how the animals buffed their walls
with their bodies to get that shine.

Most were chewed by wind
and salt water, but some held like whorled opals,
as if there are skins no element can scour.
Deep in mainland freezings, I still see
the old woman, barnacled to tides and silt,
shelling a dream for the rest of us
of flesh beneath pores, of polishing
our lives from inside out
as if no elements conspired
to shake themselves clean of us.

In the Calendar Square of the Dream

The whole square turns to ice:
It is a cube popped free
from the past's causation,
from future's effect, so that my father,
long dead, is back at the wheel
of our '49 Chevy, steering my mother,
my sister, and me on treadless tires
over the ice;
though even in the dream
we know he is dead,
we trust ourselves to his traction,

even when he jumps out
and we notice the others
jumping out, leaving hundreds of cars
free-wheeling, even when we see him
and his friends directing traffic,
pointing to chuckholes and patches
of ice, even when we see him flagging
wreckers, we are so happy to see him
back in control.

Teleportation

Thus, in every case of a strange appearance, one should look for another
of a strange disappearance.
— *Phenomena: A Book of Wonders.*

I do not speak of those
who inexplicably vanish
forever, but of those taken away
and brought back, stuttering
outlandish alibis. I think of their falling
like red rain on the farmer,
shearing his tobacco, veining the dumb vision
of cows. Or of their landing
in plaid flannel shirts
like neighbors.
But what of the ones
who step forth from the woods
leaving fur in their tracks?

Mostly I think of their being dropped,
wandering and bewildered, calling out
the names of old friends.

They remind me of lovers
who wake every day to a strange place
and try to give it a name:
home,
room left behind
by men and women who spent years
breaking it in. And drove one night
to the grocery store
for a pack of cigarettes.
Or so they intended.

Bedtime Story

If the Devil don't want nothing
he must want something.

If he ain't barely imaginable
he must be red fluorescent skin,
spikes jutting from forehead,
a shredded grin, as in *gnashing of teeth*.

If he seen you
It's too late.

But hide, hide under the covers,
may be he gets confused
in his tenses
and agreements. May be
he thinks you signed something
when you ain't signed nothing at all.

Tell him you can't hardly write.

Getting the Truth To Come Clear

"His truth is clearest when it is poised against a system of lies."
—*Mark Jarman in University Publishing*

I asked a ninety three-year-old woman,
Of everything that has happened,
what do you remember most?
She said, Once, as a child, I hid
under the porch while they rode off
on horses to find me. They got the whole county
out riding but they never came close.
When my parents grew sorry enough
I crawled out
and they went and got my cat back
from the neighbors.
Is this one measure of Truth,
I ask, the moment that leaps
across all others,
furred with consequence?

All my life I've been a sucker
for Love, Peace, as well as the darker abstractions,
have gone off after the least shreds of evidence
rumored stashed inside faces like cupboards,
awaiting my hunger. Now it is Truth
I hear will come clear
if only I choose the right backdrop.

What is the process for collecting
reliable lies? No pale equivocations:
I need the honest-to-God lies-in-the-teeth,
the indisputable deceptions, such as
"I answered your letter last week";
"My teeth are my own"; "Last night
I saw no one." I need to cover one wall
with black flannel lies
sponging light. I'll tack our photographs
there to whisper how we'll go on

forever. Then one by one
I'll move our real faces across the wall
to see what refuses absorption,
what comes clear as bone against topsoil,
for it may not be skull after all:
it may, please God, be the eyes,
or soft coils of brain;
it may be the tongue's gift

for cursing, benediction.

The Woman Who Built Her House on the Sand

I want to be here by the ocean
where nothing comes that I must learn
to love. How can anything with lessons
be love? I once knew a man
who called himself wise: he drew pictures
with fish spines on the damp sand,
saying, *heed, turn, flee.* I pressed
the whelk to my eardrum with its rush
of promises: wash away, wash away,
we will all wash away.

I have a new lover. Inside the cottage,
he oils his body for sun.
The one before made wine from dates
and pomegranates. How we loved, our skins whorling
like the insides of certain mollusks
I've collected, each time, after storm.

The ocean changes its colors, lapis–feldspar,
bdellium, manganese, and the onyx
that warns me each time to batten down.
But it is the sand that keeps me here,
because after many lives
I still cannot unriddle it as image,
composition, or simile: how is sand
like Abraham's descendants, Job's heaviness,
Solomon's largeness of mind? How is it ground
and poured into ovals I hold in my hand
and stare into?

Each time the sky blackens, the Lord's darts
needle the stilts of my cottage
toward the base of the dune.
Each time storm brews it dumps me to my knees:
I am going to die! I should have lived inland!

But each time it is the house
with my lover in it,
so instantly collapsible, scoured
from vision, as if were the heart of sand's

riddling: how am I like what remains?
Appeased, the ocean glasses over,
deadly in its terrible beauty.
I rake the beach, pocketing shards of angel wings
and abalone for my collection,
the tray I keep as proof that happiness was here,
like love, that silt is nothing
faced with memory's hold on what matters.

I will order fresh lumber.
I will take a new lover.
I will listen to the words in the whelk,
but I will not heed them.
For what if I had nothing to lose?
What if Loss had nothing in it
but the Lord's giving and taking away,
what if I slept untroubled by portents and dreams?

Even now, the sands shift under me,
open to the least brush of wind.
Last night I dreamed a sailor's turning
his back on the sea
after seeing me, in his dream,
waving and waving and waving.

For the Child Drowned in the Well of Black Water

Once I defined drowned childhood
by the child starlets I saw on TV,
fame come upon them so early
that they believed all the fan mail,
pouted when on-the-set-private tutors
pushed multiplication tables,
pitched fits if off-stage mothers
fixed tuna fish for lunch.

The day your mother brought you to me
she marked an X where her name should have filled
the blank granting permission for field trips;
Welcome, Teresa, come in, I said, offering a hug
you backed off from so fast
I saw the outstretched arm
must speak differently to each of us.

You spoke to no one for months.
How many days I hid you in the bathroom
pinching nits from your hair, bathing you
in warm sink water, pinning a ribbon
in your strawed hair, erasing what I could
of your smell of acrid, dried urine. You never spoke
but grinned, baring all your rotten teeth, knowing
that for one day, no one would shove his chair
away from you, no chants of "she stinks"
would machete the wax in your eardrum.

When you finally talked
I found myself praying you wouldn't,
that I would miss some minimal bliss
of ignorance. You talked about fathers,
how yours walked in brand new every week, sometimes
two or three times in one day,
and that once a father who stayed a whole month
actually learned your name
and brought you a book of paper dolls
you still slept with, having never snipped
them from their backgrounds of slick whiteness.

My one hope was that you were a pathological
liar. But you weren't, and then how I needed
to teach you of other rooms
some people grow up to live in,
where supper is often tuna or a cheap grade
of ground beef, but doors are left open
for entries, exits, some approximation of love.

When all the other children were way beyond names,
could mimic Dog, Cat, Snake, any shape of holiday,
all you gave me were sheets filled with Ts aimed
in all directions. All this high purpose of mine
failed so long ago that some nights I can barely
remember your face. I try not to ask
if you have a new collection of fathers
all of whom know you by name
for one night, and leave ten dollars
on the table for the privilege.
If so I hate them most of all
because they use a name
you never wrote on a page where Ts collided,

a page I still hold
in shaking hands as if fingers could braille
the secret of how you have come to be
whoever you are,
as if I could go to your mirror and stare
until glass melts into a well
of black water, where objects take turns
floating up to the surface—dolls, jump ropes,
skates, a grosgrain ribbon, a snag-toothed grin,

then plummet for their third and final drowning.

Poem for the Tick

We never hear him drop
from a leaf or pine needle
onto one pore. While we're camping out
he's camping in where our skin closes
like tent flaps.

Hard-shelled, he bloats like any poacher
with no heart for his own blood
while ours pumps like a lover
loving only himself. We want
to pick him off before he bloats
with connections to the brain.
Even after checks of our scalps
we're sure he's still attached.

the heavy hidden drinker in all of us.
the real reason our hairs turn gray
and the skull sets up camp
behind our faces.

Something Good on the Heels of Something Bad

When things get too bad, as they usually do,
I try to remember the friend who told me
"troubles are money in the bank."
She should have known,
and if I go outside
it is not to run from a pack of dogs,
breaking my leg on ice;
it is not to crunch through the snow
to Broad Street and talk again to the man
who wheels himself into the bar
at the end of each day; it is not to hear him
say, "tomorrow's take will be better";
it is not to watch the bartender extend his credit.

I do not go out
to run into the ghost of my grandmother,
wringing her pale hands, asking
why I am all that is left
of her green chromosomes, complaining
of insufficient compensation.

There are authentic accounts
of reversals: last week I met a man
who'd lost his job, his wife, his children
and just when he'd given up hope,
he won the lottery,
his father left him a farm in Minnesota,
and a woman he liked even better showed up.

Look out, my friend said,
if nothing's missing,
if everyone you love has all his parts.
Look out if sky floats full of cumulus.
And sometimes, she said, when things are bad
they have to get worse, much worse,
before sorrow is torn into scraps of redeemable paper.

I am going out in this blizzard
to track the bright sides of drifts,

of wheels spun loose into ditches.
I am going out to listen for the beast
that comes sniffing at the heels of bad news.
I have to believe he's out there, that

he's already picked up the scent
of crushed will, heartsblood, that any moment
I will hear him eating the awful evidence.

Tending

It's no secret I've failed
with all our gardens. There were the tiger-lily bulbs
I never split that died of strangulation,
the roses with skeleton leaves,
the chrysanthemums with fungus,
and always the centipede grass with its root system
of runners.

So much you think you yank up
goes on with its underground tunnels
siphoning water and sun,
feeling for another nudgable crumb of dirt.

My children, I need to tend you more carefully
than gardens. When we moved here, deadnettle and thistle
had already taken over and it was almost a relief
to throw up my hands, say,
"All is lost," and turn inward.
And some things have happened to me
that have made me feel we have no more chance
than stems left to choke and rot,
that the only roots will be those tunnels
sucking us into the earth.

But I will never tell you.
Because maybe the yard is outside,
not connected to us, maybe weeds take over
everything but us. Maybe,
just because I fail in weeding out
my own duplicities, leaving them to run riot
all over my body, it doesn't mean
I can't learn some saving pull for you,
my arms towing you in over deep water.

The possibility alone keeps me reaching.

Losing Rings

You blame me for losing my rings,
three in five years.
I say, "My fingers lose weight with loving."
I too have wondered at the ease
with which they slid off undetected:
one into dirt my hands dug out for bulbs,
another into river,
and one I last saw pulling sleeves
from a laundromat dryer.

None had enough scratches to be a symbol
for unending love, so when I think about them,
I do not think of gold circumferences
but of the space inside and what fills it:
somewhere dirt, muck on river bottom,
lint in a stranger's pocket
are the finger I should have grown,
the one I keep trying to fatten
or if nothing else works, coat with glue.

Finally you turn to me, empty-handed,
saying, Here is the ring of imagination,
imagine love that goes on forever,
imagine this is the last ring you will be given,
imagine anything you need to make it fit.

My fingers are nearly all bone.
But I imagine a ring shrinking like skin.

Thinking of Others

My mother's solution
for my father's depression:
Think of others worse off than you.
And for each step he took with his walker
she found a man with no legs,
no wheelchair, no woman to pull him back
from the brink.

For each hold he couldn't keep on a saucer
she knew a man with hands blown off
in a factory explosion.

When the numbness spread to his tongue,
she reminded him of the camp
where prisoner's tongues were lit or cut out.

For each face he could no longer make out,
there were babies born blind,
dumped in trashcans.
There was Helen Keller.
There was the man with two heads
growing right out of his spine.

She knew people with none of their parts
who kept going.
For each feeling my father lost
she offered him Pain
and what it could feel like
if he could feel.

Poem for Exchange of Habitat

There is always something outside
that wants in: again tonight,
I cannot back the car out of the garage
for the animals that gather. I think
of moving back to the city,
where not once did I choke
on the spray of wild skunk
on my path to the dryer, not once
did I intercept the nocturnal missions
of cats, possums, dogs. What is this pull

towards the hum of my machines, toward
tables, sleeves, flesh, lamplight,
flicked-down dark? When they move up close,
the home that bounced off their eyes
is one I cannot give them,
though my own stares twisting these hills
prove my willingness to trade
our Lists-of-What-Is-Denied.

Why else would I sit up so late
writing letters to the dead
or vanished? I seal them and carry them out
to their box by the roadside, hoist
the red flag and wait. I know
they are out there, re-estimating
the contents, sizing the exchange.

The Clothesline Body

Each night I leave my dress on the line
between the Sumacs.
I unbutton the bodice and cuffs
so the dark can fall in easily,
taking my body's place
without the limits my hands
put on reach, my feet put on movement,
my head puts on knowing and loving.

This body's mouth fills with fireflies
and leaves, a broth of lichen,
mothwings. This body's hair is so long
it wafts the hills. Part of it lies
in the creek, filling with mayflies
and algae. A crayfish cracks out of its shell
and hides under a rock in my eardrum.
My tongue turns into wind.

Mornings, I go out and put on the dress,
buttoning it clear to the neck and wrists,

and wake the children with the touch
that barely knows where it's been.

Hot Bath in an Old Hotel

Asleep, you turn
on the knots in your neck
though I spent an hour
ironing your back with my knuckles.
We stiffen with travel.
I take off my clothes
and sit on the cold porcelain bottom
of the tub. I want it like this,
my spine stabbed and chilled
as a column of ice cubes.
Look, I can take it, I hiss
through my teeth, through the door.

I turn the handle
and lie back as water
scalds its way up like memories.
With each inch I lose a sadness.
By the time it reaches my neck,
I have forgotten who we are.

Callers

I accidentally dial
my own number.
The line is busy.
I wonder to whom
my friend talks
at this hour.
Then the digits
jingle like coins from slots
in my brain, and I know
I am calling myself.
I do not hang up
for five minutes.

Last week, I made
a similar mistake,
dialing my empty house
from a pay phone.
It rang one time
before I slammed the receiver
in panic,
certain that at any moment
the I
I left home
would answer, saying,
have a good time,
don't hurry back,
everything's waxed,
supper's simmering
without you.

For months
we have answered the phone
to heavy breathing.
The children are afraid;
my husband wants
an unlisted number.
Only I
feel relief
in pressing my ear

to someone else's
respiratory system.
Relief that I am not
the dialer,
that there is more
to this business
of contact
than overhearing the self
through busy signals,
more than leaving
oneself inside walls
only to panic
that she is the one
who inherits.

The caller
chose our number
out of millions.

Against such odds
I hang on
until he hangs up.

Fifty calls, and still
our breaths' timing is wonderfully
off. Our exhalations intersect
spasmodically.
We are not two
of a kind.

Shared Visions

"Our interest is in visions which are perceived by more than one person,
and we are content to leave the explanations to others."
                    —*Phenomena: A Book of Wonders*

Often more than one sees:
the rope standing on its end,
the boy shimmying up it
becoming a cloud; the ship
that lands in Kansas,
glowing all night in a field.

Those who see cannot help
but marry each other.

Years go by.
He still thinks of the night
a blue fog with hands and feet
walked on the water.
She remembers it as a lantern
swinging in the grip
of a drowned sailor.
Some nights it's the ascensions
of wings through the roof.
Some nights it's that woman in black
you could put your hand through
and promise never to forget.

Concerning A Dog Hit in Backwoods Tennessee

Only a moment ago, you were thinking
how, despite the everywhere hills,
their peaks and pits seemed negotiable,
as if someone had taken the time
to pour them from a slow truck,
working with the tumbling rhythm
of the part of Earth that decided, Here all
will be headed up or down, and always know which,
leaving guess and surmise
to riders of flat stretches through desert, coastline.

The scenery, you'd have said,
was picturesque, a background for a painting
which kept to its place, allowing you
your God-given space as a focal point
in foreground; at most, one or two
twister-whipped pines, rocks, blades of rye grass
may have leaned toward you
as if wanting more deeply into the blur
of your attention. Only afterwards
do you remember this and try to guess
what might have happened had you stopped
to hear their versions of what wind had done
to them, along with downpours, droughts, late freezes.
Look at us: we are not as we were
and somehow we want you to notice our becoming
something else, for whether blessing or curse,
this is the way we keep happening.

But that would have taken more than you could spare
of a shortening life. Then: Dog. Fur the color
of the parched field-weeds it burst from
to leap at your car, and you not knowing
who it was
that slammed your brakes, skidded into ditch
after the dull thump
of dog suddenly lying in your rearview mirror's
inadequate patch of hindsight.

Struck dumb as stone-brain, you sense only
that something must be done: what is one's duty
here? Grim tales of those who spin getaways
in rubber. *Help*, you say to anything
that might listen. Climbing out, with only one foot
on pavement, you watch in disbelief
dead dog rising, shaking tire-tracks from fur,
loping across field as if transfused
with stallion blood.

All this took place so long ago
that it seems very late
for you to still be asking, What happened?
But you do,
and one answer may be
once a dog ran into you
out of instinct, madness, or unignorable orders.
The meaning of blood and dent
you cannot beat from fender
is not clear, except that it is
clearly not related to guilt,
as you were on your way to attempting the right
thing, and there is no dog left
on hyphenated lines to be run down again
and again, becoming tread for tires, nightmares.

No one can tell you if what
by now maybe limps with pain
or lies in a swoon of guts
chose you out of so many travelers,
a wild thing bent on collision, wreckage,
ancient memory trace
in which a mound of dry bones
must precede each resurrection.

No one can tell you how this will turn out
or if what darts in and out
deserves your serious attention.

Perhaps it is only the first
in a long list of encounters,
preparation for mastering the skill
of trusting yourself again to steering
what it becomes.
or sleep with the scantest information,
of leaving more than you ever dreamed
unfinished, up in air, becoming
what it becomes.

At the Wharf, Yorktown: For All Tracks Made in Sand

Because this is a July night,
more sunbathers have vanished
than in January, leaving only tracks
like clues traffic-jamming the whole length of beach.

If I were a better liar
I would swear I have come
searching for the feet of true direction,
lost while ambling north by south,
sideways by transistor radio,
snatched straight up into sky.

But this beach is no abstraction
On a real night in October
I walked here, in love again
with love
who wore a green leisure suit
who wore eyes like the ocean
who wore a mouth that told me,

over lobster dinner, how this
was what he'd waited for all his life:
(Yes, this is what we wait for
all of our lives.)
Afterwards, we dug for augers,
drill-shells that bore into sand
as soon as they're dumped by the ocean,
each packed with one microscopic blot
of poison, barely enough
to put an amoeba to sleep.
Nor are the augers abstractions:
we filled our pockets, took them home,
strung them into necklaces as proof.

How many real days in April
found me here, in love again
with love
who wore cut-offs
who wore eyes that bounced my face

off his prescription lenses,
who wore a mouth that told me,
over cheese-and-cracker lunch,
how he had never known anything like this.
(Each time we have never known
anything like this.)
Afterwards we scooped augers
into our jeans; back home I filled a Mason jar
(augers are useless as ashtrays)
with evidence.

Some parts of these stories
are lies. Fossilized, what will our tracks
prove to archaeologists? Tonight
is a real night in July
and I am here alone
in love again
with love
who wears air
shifting across a million mismatched
shoes. When I address you, Love,
stand in one place until I'm finished—
Who gave you permission to bear
all your faces
into the heart of swept dunes?

Love, I think I am coming to know you
through your infinite directions, your series
of practice drills, perfecting each march
into the heart by training on sand:
no wonder we never hear you come in.

This is what we wait for
all of our lives. Each time
we have never known anything like it.
This digging for augers,
this turn and return,

these cupped palms aching to be filled.

For My Mother, Feeling Useless

Some people grow chalky dust on their skin
like leaves on a dirt road.
My Mother, who would not run to the drugstore
without clean underwear, stockings,
hair pinned, two spots of blusher,
who believed everything mattered,
now sighs, *no need, no need.*

Who am I? she asks
of my father's, my sister's, and my faces
on the wall, under glass.
Her face lies on them
until it cannot bear the likenesses.

If she goes out for supper
no one knows if she comes back
or keeps driving
into the ocean
or down a dirt road spraying dust.

On her last plane ride
she had a vision
of being taken up
beyond the top cloud;
then she heard a voice
telling her she had to go
down, she was needed.

When I was a child,
she owned two dresses,
many aprons. There was great need
for her hands in the sink,
in the threadbox with needles.

There was great need
when my grandfather's brain
turned to mush, when my father lost
his sense of touch.

I leave my house
and go down the clay road
where the trees smother
into ghosts of themselves.
A car spins past, coating my legs
with gravelly powder
and I warn, *Back off, dark space,*
I've got connections.
My husband and children saw me leaving.

We Never Get to the End of It All

Even when I think we're at the end,
crates of clothes and mementos packed,
there is still my great-grandmother
laid out in the tintype,
hands folded across the bosom
of her Sunday dress, waiting
for her likeness. Ahead there's a man
with his head inside a black curtain,
flashing a pan of light. Off to the side,
my grandmother, twelve, is wooed
by a muslin apron, its deep pockets
where the hands, shirking burdens, might hide.
Air stalls for its moment
and passes. The man packs his equipment
in saddlebags and rides off.
My grandmother sits by the bed all day,
all night. Later she will place the tintype
face down in her lap, scratching a nail's vow
into metal: *I will never have a child.*

Leftovers

When the mind thinks of leaving
suddenly the good things rise
like calm, communicative children
misplaced in a classroom
of autistics. How we love them,
dragging their patches of light
across our yard. How we stare
at these children
who enter all our metaphors,
each one lit with his aura of lostness,
each one flaring for his moment
in memory, saying, *Wait, this signifies.*

And there is the non-metaphorical child
whose coffin was dug up,
ten years in the ground,
and still there was something,
something to dust.

Middle Age

The groundhog we dumped in the woods
is back in the yard
where he lies with his head in a cloud
of lice, an aura of flies,
a pale apple-green shimmering.

You say the dogs bring him back,
wanting praise, claiming credit.
At first I thought him but one more proof
of Spring, like wasps in vents,
ticks in children. All I know is he's there
when I walk to the mailbox,
when I lie in the sun,
when I look up at the stars
to say we're all nearer
to each other than we are.

He's a message from my father,
refusing to settle with the dead,
warning me I lack the skills
to keep them buried. Something's trying
to keep me from grief, but I'm not fooled:
love doesn't come back
like this, nor second chance.

Children gather to poke the remains,
then go fishing. I'm left
where the dead and the young
would keep me, cleaning up the mess.
What a mess they leave.

Girl Passing Among Trailers

She is maybe eleven, twelve,
though you have to be so young here
not to have had sex
she seems younger.
Then, barefoot, in yellow shorts
and a blouse loose
as a mother's, sister's, she walks out,
crosses the mud-gravel road
toward another trailer,
where someone is calling
or crying. She goes in , comes out
pushing a small child in a stroller.
She maneuvers among loose, bony dogs,
the garbage they've chewed to trash
and scattered across all the yards.
She steers between blankets
where two other girls lie,
blistering, their babies napping fitfully
in a playpen.

It is Spring in the treeless, grass-less
trailer court, though you have to look askance
for signs of urge, surge, prime, burst,
flourish: clumps of dandelion, chickweed
where wheels would be
if these houses moved
as they were meant to; girls oiling
their stretch marks, turning
and turning, as though sun
were all their Spring this year
and from now on.

This is not where each was going
this time last year, when she stared at sky
for all that was about to happen—
the rock music, the boy, the flight
into lives free from parents. At least
that's what they say

to the girl pushing the stroller:
Don't fall for some guy,
Don't get married
Let us be a lesson,
You'll find out!

I am the cloudy plastic window
she walks past to enter
my daughter's trailer
saying *Let me, Let me.*
Boil my grandson's water.
Give him a bath, change his diaper.
Changing him, she showers talc
like silk rain
into the folds of flesh,
the creases of tiny arms that reach
to be held, to hold.
She dresses him, cooing, You smell
so good, You so soft, want to go
for a ride? Let me take him home
with me, the girl begs my daughter,
who says not today, my mother doesn't get
here often. Bereft, she continues her rounds

in widening concentrics, circling
her shapes of longing
and pleasure through the trailer park
as though straining against her own fullness
of ignorance, bliss.

To the House Ghost

Just because I turn on the light
it doesn't mean I don't want you around.
I know how you like to keep your own
shredded space among hangers and vents;
you think I have no room for you
at the table or in bed. But listen:
I have made room in my ribcage more than once.
There is always something that wants to move over
to borrow air like trouble.

You could light my cigarettes.
After I'm in bed, lean over my impossible wishes
and blow them out. Lie down and tell me
who cut you down in your prime,
decribe the weapon.

Being Refused Local Credit

Too new in town, we're told
though we give twenty years
of references, debts owed
and paid, companies that begged
us as risks. How long does it take,
I ask, am told, Years.
OK, I shrug to my husband; so we'll pay cash.
But my heart's not in it,
knowing how everything it ever wanted arrived
before the wherewithal,
how without the foolhardy trust
of certain friends and strangers
I'd have had nothing, nothing.

This may be the town I'll learn
to be good in, filled with counters, aisles
where my credit's no good and my hands
stay in my pockets, counting costs.

Suddenly we don't need
almost everything. For years
we're too new
to be trusted; We're back
in those barracks-turned-apartments
before our first child:
We're reading *1984* in paperback, taking turns

reading aloud the passages that seem most possible,
war and loneliness and rats.
The daughter we can't pay for
takes all this in, with our screams and yelling and rock
        music;
the tiny clot of heart muscles contracts,
perusing. . . .

You're working overtime,
not enough. If it's day shift
I sweep, huge-bellied, where I can,
visit the woman next door
who seems to me so wise
with grown children.
If third shift, I bolt-lock the doors,
sit up half the night
with a butcher knife
as you told me, asking
Who would want to steal from us? Who?

The New Tenants in Our Old Duplex

In the garage, over their car,
swallows's nests drip
spittle and a paste of weeds, twigs,
droppings; upstairs, by their bedroom
window, a pair of starlings line a mud cup
in the box air-conditioner,
and all morning it sounds
like boiled eggs
popping, after the water's run
out, the pot's still on the burner
on high.

If he shaves by the bathroom mirror
he shaves lips, ears,
eyesight. She combs long undulations
of face.

And the phone rings once or twice
for Rankin, they don't live here.
Or sometimes it rings
and no one asks for anyone.
Who's this? Who's this? Who's this?

Their dog finds new times
for barking, new reasons.

Two Ways of Listening to Rain

That April morning, the sycamore had opened its leaves
like plates, it wanted rain so. We opened our mouths
like bowls, wanting what we could not name,
the tongue newly afloat in its silver
inarticulation. Tonight a steady rain
has fallen for hours, pestling my yard
with fallen leaves; walking through the certainties
of mulch, I can steady my tongue
to say backwards, Ah, yes, regeneration!
We wanted to live again! To know, through our palms,
how leaves must rush at their first green shock
of chlorophyll. Lonely man, I think I hear you
alone in your tower, listening to rain,
saying it's time for the dead
to bury the dead. I think I hear
you saying the butter-yellow maple
is drained and umbered
from what you remember. You speak
of diminishing,
having learned nothing from seasons and their selfish,
magnificent gestures: It's my turn, they say, Move over.
I hear them in this rain
on slick paths of leaves
where balance begins
 and the wind sounds like water rushing
inside tree trunks
or inside wrists
if we could hear ourselves
pounding.

Stigmata

". . . many genuine and devout recipients would conceal them, or pray
that they might suffer the pain but show no outward sign of the wound
to excite the curious."
            –Phenomena: A Book of Wonders

More than the saint
who fasted
for a cross
 to come slashing its love
for his hand
 are those whose irises burn
in least light,
whose eardrums collapse
at a whisper.

More than those who pray in public
are those who appear to be shaking
 only from cold, who ask
for a closet.

Something wants to describe
itself on skin, to explain
why the bleeding heart is,
must be. Something else
dreads attention, hiding
in a rash
beneath a wedding band,
under eyelids.

There are more
who are quiet.
Many more
who are very quiet.

Webs

By September, we cannot move through the yard
without tearing whole networks
of tracery down.
It's been a long time since I've been trapped
by lies this intricate and silken,
and I lie down in the grass
to see if it's all really spun from one's body
like angel hair, each careful knot
an alibi shot with sunlight–
the spinner paused here, here, and here.

My grandmother was married
forever. She took her broom
and swept clothesline, trees, and house
free of spiders' and hearts' entanglements.
She whisked great plans
from the veins of leaves and children.
She moistened thread on the tip of her tongue
and sewed sleeves back onto shoulders
and died mistrusting anyone's account
of whereabouts.

Glossolalia

Downstairs, women are speaking
in tongues. I do not understand them,
but as the warbled, garbled syllables rise,
it's just as hard
not to imagine
each tongue's reaching new bars
of music, each head's sputtering licks
of clarifying flame,
as to believe
in the hopelessness of speech
or in atmosphere that bears our words
to blue heavens, where we'll spend eternity
taking them back.

It was just as difficult not to believe
my father was a messenger from God
as to swallow his messages. Aphasiac at the end,
he stammered a language of letting go,
a radical phonics of reconnections,
his tongue breaking
through thickets of loss
to rename the world's parts with absolute
imperfection. When I laid my head
on his chest, I heard a wind
rasping dry leaves, consonants swept like trash,
tracks, trouble from a room I did not want
to lie in,
a room where, years later,
my daughter and I would drop
to our knees in an anguish
of incoherencies, our single agreement
on links between blood,
betrayal, allegiance, judgement, mercy,
children, mothers, screaming,
an agreement she never speaks of,
cleaning her house, tending her child.
A covenant like a room swept,
moved out of, words like nail holes
new tenants plaster over
until even the absences inside them are lost.
She could be a woman after my own dumb heart,

now that, more than anything, I want to call her,
tell her how,
when I was eighteen, a boy I loved
was killed; every night for a month
two friends and I lit candles,
balanced a Ouija board on our knees,
asked it questions.
Every night for a month
something answered.
I later thought, *knees, fingers,*
oscillations of brain, heart's throb
for connections.

But if I was wrong,
if they were souls,
they believed in God
but were not with him.
It was dark there, unimaginably crowded,
and lonely.
Call it Robert, John, Martha, father,
sister, lover
it would come
spelling *Yes.*
Anything to hold
attention,
anything not to be
air
or countlessness
of stars, angels.
Hours later I could still feel the graze
of fingertips against the plastic triangle
pulling me down the alphabet,
my true love's leaning like curvature
of time, space, breathing.
Now I think we were calling ahead
to ourselves *Whither?* and call back,
Choose me. But if I am wrong

lost souls are more in love
with our voices and hands
than we imagine, and
 so lonely that when bored, exhausted
with their world, we'd spell *Goodbye,*
the triangle would slide
out from under our fingers to *No.*

Unreasonable Footprints

Sometimes we wake to a yard of them,
scars gouged deep in mud
 as barrow pits, reminders of how much circles,
walks up to have a look
without letting us know.

Then the inevitable lantern and hound,
nights we stalk these fields with neighbors
to flush the mystery, to fill holes with an eyewitness account,
to come back with a name for the vanished,
something with fur, real blood, a scent.

I never tell you how I love the not knowing,
those moments when we wallow in our ignorance
and the trespasser is anything it needs to be
to get attention. I like to think it's the Possibility
for love, puzzling the moves it should make,

not knowing enough
to come in our of the rain. Or these auras
of absences out bodies are said to emanate:
I like to think the vanished go on inside them,
that above "Goodbye" hovers a print whose owner

even air cannot help but shape itself around.
Most of all I think of entering that moment
before the foot, poised over all possible tracks,
begins to come down, before desire chooses
its avenue to memory through us,

harrowing the darkness between like clods of warm earth.

Somewhere Else

The waitress
takes our order, but clearly
her mind is
            somewhere else–

It's one of those days,
she says, handing us drinks
for someone else's thirst
which we forgive, though even our forgiveness
interrupts a conversation
            somewhere else–

Our roast burns
for a man across town,
a thankless child,
bad luck, no money
customers full of unlikelihoods
here, possibilities
there–

And in our children's eyes
we see the meal we've bought them
go cold, so impatient are they
to be already
where they're going,
spinning rubber down a driveway
where houselights are just beginning to come on,
it's just beginning to be dark.

Goldfinches at the Nuclear Plant

You draw me a picture
and ask me to imagine yellow,
black, in undulating
interchange, stripes chopped
from a flag in stiff wind.

But I cannot see
anything, much less birds,
as I walk, before sunrise
from the parking lot down the clay road
following bootprints in the mud
banked up to the Employee Entrance.
Nor can I believe
as the time clock punches
and I file behind others
past sheet rock walls the yellow
of yellow teeth, yellow toenails, yellow snow.

There are no windows here.
I must wait to meet you at lunch
in the field where the cooling tower looms
like a Martian condominium. We break
simple bread under what looks like
simple sky, though complicated with wishing,
waiting, and we stumble onto evidence:
cups of grass, reed strips, spittle,
gold feathers graying into weeds
by the creek bank. It's winter;
goldfinches were here, and are gone.
I imagine one whose feathers I hold
stuttering wings through sky
over Key West, the Gulf, Guatemala,

and as with everything
that doesn't seem to belong,
these winter sunsets like chilled
blackberry currant poured
into white wine, black traceries
of trees like those a welder, in his secret life,

cuts out with scissors so small
they are lost in his hand,
I want to eat the feathers
or graft their down onto shoulder blades
or pin them to my hair
as I go back inside the building
after lunch. I want the woman beside me
to look up from her documentation
and think, *flight*,
the man across from me to defect
from technician reports, jump onto his desk.
astonish our air with arm-flapping.

But the feathers stay in my pocket
kept from the woman who limps in
every Monday bruised, welted,
the man with eight mouths beyond his,
all hungry, the supervisor whose wife
has cancer, no insurance,
kept from everyone
who does not belong here

but will lumber, years after I'm gone,
through pre-dawn in steel-toed shoes,
shapes lost inside hooded down,
not thinking
one more month of this,
thinking of migrations
only as moves to new job sites,
dark-to-dark hours everywhere,

as grunt, silence, cold
that enter my pre-walking
bearing a darkness
like their forever
I have only been a part of.

Making Tracks

I'm leaving again,
passing through the gate by the cows
heading down the dirt road
with my arms thrown open to air–
I've had such trouble breathing.

I'm going to stake a tent
in the weeds and forget pretending
 the house suffers
as we do, that walls weep
over a child's fever, that doors are pleased
when we enter. Goodbye to acquienscence,
that pale ghost that lets dust settle
like slipcovers over bodies.

I know this dirt road by heart,
can smell my way down it by thistle,
 ragweed. I know exactly where the doberman
is locked in his pen behind the barn,
exactly how much of his mouth is higher
than the fence, exactly the moment my scent
siphons growl
from a deep well in his throat.

This road winds its dusty ellispse
over a path cows must have chosen,
needing endlessness. I know where the road
turns back on itself, where I always lie down
to stare at the sky until it takes my anger.
But this time it's not working:
it's taking longer for fear to whip rage,
to picture the house on the hill
with lamps on at dusk,

the people inside well-fed, leaning
toward happiness like sleep.

It's not fair that a child
always enters this picture,
his face blanched as moonlit field.
Is that what keeps the road
doubling back, having children?
I close my eyes and see you bent,
salvaging tomato plants
from the cutworm's nightly slash
at the base of each stem,
as close to the ground
fingers can't get under,
and I know, No, it's something else,
something. I wonder what happens
in a dog's brain when she's run through fields
all day and starts home,
never thinking, *home*,
only choosing the same door
from so many. A quiet dog, she leaps onto our sofa
and sleeps. We find her on her side,
her legs scooping and shoving air
as if they were still in a field.

Preservatives

The night the ocean froze in Virginia
we walked with lanterns
on top of the breakers, listening in disbelief
to the silence. I knelt,
searched for fish and periwinkles
embedded at split moments of turning:
you found bird tracks pricked
on the swell of a wave.

How I loved you.
I thought of ferns on fossilized slate,
of people packed in storage
until a later century's
necessary miracle of scientists
who'd chip them out,
teaching unimaginable transitions.

Above us, winter birds, crying *hurry, hurry,*
flocked further south.

Twenty years, and I taste salt
when I shake you over memory.

Some nights I cry out your name
through trees, toward sky,
and the wind comes behind,
sweeping. It doesn't know what to do
when it meets you: it thinks of a bird,
a leaf, a compromise with all the shapes
that shape it. Then it remembers.
No; I am the wind.

Here

For the first time
I pull your death up
onto paper and write
Bullet through the lung.
It was our first Sunday night
in the new house, my first
a thousand miles from you.
My husband had brought a grate,
screen, tongs, hearth-broom, ash-shovel,
bellows to keep air
burning. Watching him, watching fire,
I let myself feel
I'd moved far enough
to be good. The phone rang.
A voice told me
of an accident, a gun
not even meant for you.
The voice had held you last,
it had last cradled your head in its hands,
 and I didn't recognize it.

I had to pretend it was
nothing. I remember going down
steep, dark stairs
to the basement to put a load
in the dyer. I remember
the washing machine's chipped lid
as it held me up
with both hands, my mouth
opening and closing, something
refusing to rise from the well
behind my molars, my throat
like a sink drain clogged with hair
and dental floss.

My second feeling: *Traitor,* you've left me
the whole burden of memory.

I read Proust for a year, starring
every other paragraph, writing

Amens in the margins. I remember thinking,
maybe he's right,
maybe five years down the road
I'll be someone I barely know,
full of fresh brain and skin cells,
all the zillions
where you'd touched me
long sloughed into atmosphere's
swirling *Who?*

That night, standing over the washer's
well, I unknotted sleeves, pants,
bedsheets. I could see
I was going to need a desperate
patience, I could see to get here
we were going to have to take
enormous breaths.

Requiem

Almost at the awful end of us,
our unmusical son
tries to build musical instruments
from scraps–aluminum foil, rusty funnel,
rubber bands, broken combs.
The apartment is rife with his failures

but this is a physics project, required, so
he keeps gluing, stretching, tearing, strumming,
blowing. He blusters though the hole
in a long-playing record he's taped to a bowl,
straining to be a tuba. You leave
to wash a car. I want to run after,
tell you something, strum the mouth
of our terrible silence. While you're gone

he goes in the field among needlerush, wild
oat reeds. Crouching by bases of stems,
he chooses one, slices it aslant, blows
through its tunnel of absence.

Last week, you walked out in blizzard
to listen in that field, learning the rabbit's,
the sparrow's fierce shelters, returning
blue-lipped, babbling.

Our son wheezes though the reed, but nothing
comes out. He pokes holes through the top; it splits
along its fibrous fault lines. He throws it

aside, turns to percussion, echoes.
I wanted you to be here
the moment I looked up to see him
in the field: right before sundown, whole
bowls of ochre light poured into valley, down
the west sides of hills, weeds, boy. Then the world
turned rose, mauve, the colors of earth
mixed with vermilion, saffron, sky.
I dreamed that light into a huge
sadness, knowledge, forgiveness,
a final tenderness intoning all
we've withheld from each other.

It was an excruciatingly
beautiful light. But late,
very late.

Divorce: A Romance

It's July, 1961. We're leaning across opposite sides
of the counter. I'm sixteen and so dumb, hungry, unlovely
no one will ever choose me. I'm listening
to your Air Force stories, your landings
all over the world. I've never been
out of Newport News, Virginia, and this is my first job,
frying hamburger patties, slicing onions. I'm so thin
you can't see me sideways. You live downtown
in a boarding house, work third shift in the Shipyard.
For days now you've tossed you hard hat on the counter,
I've filled you order, you've gulped it down.
You tell me I'm pretty, we ride around town
in your Cheverolet, we ride to Ocean View, we
ride all the way to Richmond. I'm fired from my job.
our songs are "Love is Strange," "I Couldn't Sleep
at All Last Night," and "Duke of Earl,"

but you can't dance

or carry a tune, and we've run out of places
to ride, and we cannot imagine that anyone else
will ever love us

so we marry.

Then everything happens: birthdays, anniversaries, children,
deaths, grandchildren; our lives–almost anyone's.
So why do I keep trying to get back to those children
we were? So young, so stupid, they stare through me,
shivering toward us. I want to yank them.
out of the car, fell them *one of you will die!* But they keep
reaching for each other, absences, betrayals, fury.
You're going to ruin your lives! I scream at them,

but they're so needy

who knows how their story will end? She's so
immature. He's such a Romantic. Their parents married young

and forever, who had nothing,
nothing in common.

Dove in a Sycamore

The mourning dove, her feathers the color
of tree bark and this January rain,
doesn't know she sounds sad, much less
how her moans and ooos call out

those far places inside us,
absences, losses, and bring them home
beneath her wings. It must have been beautiful.
How magnificently we must have loved

to feel so grieved now, so bereft.
And all this while we've thought our love
paltry, parsimonious, never rising fully
to its occasions. But one pre-dawn morning

we're sitting alone in a car
in a parking lot, waiting for buildings
to unlock, for others to come help us
start up the world, when the dove,

from her low limb, will not stop crying.
How pure our flight into each love
must have been, how those pieces of sky
must still air the sweat beneath our armpits,

how lovely we must have all been.

How Much

Enough that I wish
it were 1954, both of us children
in the same small town. We're sealing
tiny crabs in a jar; we're too young to know
we're killing them. Hurricane Hazel comes through
and among dozens of uprooted poplars
we fight over who gets which rooms.

Enough that if you inherit Alzheimer's,
your father's disease, I will remain in your skull
and dance darkly, freely with the others.
set loose from the moorings
of memory. I will dive into that pond
to the bottom of the lily's thick, thorned root
and sleep, sleep.

Enough that I wish we were
dreary, with all our words worn
thin and out, with one of us staring out the window
for all sky rumored it would bring us,
the other asleep in front of the TV.
Enough to be given years
to turn into each other

like the old man and woman
I watch walking every night
to their own syncopation, two feet, four
meeting the ground as they need to,
hovering their split-seconds in air
as they need to
above all their futures

and all that comes calling behind.
Enough that tonight, packing,
I wish above all things
you were the dull, true man
napping on the den sofa
who will love me forever, the man
I am about to betray.

Luck: West Side Market, Cleveland

The pregnant, blue-scarfed woman in yellow anklets
comes into the market to get warm, drink coffee,
eat breadcrust someone left on the counter
by the pay phone. When the man comes in
she starts dialing and dialing.
You got no quarter, he says.
Lemme alone, she says; *I toldja lemme alone.*
Between thumb and forefinger, she pinches
nothing, drops it into the coin slot, dials,
starts talking, crying to her mother
who must be saying, *Not now, I'm busy*
or *Come home.* The man hangs up the phone,
pulls the woman away. When he opens the door
all the hand-written "Wanted" and "Lost" ads
flail from thumbtacks; her scarf flares from her head
like phosphor as he drags her into wind
down the icy street. Everyone standing in this corner
of the market–man weighing prime rib, waitress
wiping counters, man browsing through magazines,
and I, a woman trying to stay warm, staring
through the door's steamed glass for you–
see, hear this, do nothing. *Lemme alone,*
the woman hisses, then is gone.
What if I ran after, found her shelter?
In a moment the door re-opens
and they're back. *Lemme alone,* she says. He drops
nothing into the phone, dials her mother,
says, *She hung up.* They go outside,
then come back. They pool everything they have
and call everyone's mother, father, sister, brother, child,
friend, acquaintance, stranger. No one answers.
They go out, they come in, they go out. The door
opens, closes, opens. *Just lemme alone,* she keeps saying
through clattering teeth. He doesn't let her alone.
They go in and out. Each time the door opens
the ads flap, wave, shiver; my skirt flies over my knees.
None of us does anything to thwart this. You stand
beside me ten minutes before I remember
who we are, why we've come here.

Mantises

I'm sitting on the back stoop
with someone I barely know
when a mantis leaps over my shoulder
to a stone bordering a plot of cosmos,
nasturtiums, asters. It's November,
and the mantis' body is so busy turning
into Other–blanched leaf, stubble, stone–
that she pays no attention to us.
It doesn't help that I've just left
a long marriage, or that yesterday,
through my study window,
I watched my next-door neighbor
digging a hole for what I thought
was a tree. But he brought a black bag
the size of his dog
to the hole, dropped it in, shoveled dirt,
tamped and tamped. It doesn't help
that the bindweed beyond my desk window
knots, bulbs as if it were April.
In April, I kept a mantis egg case
inside my office terrarium, screened it over,
brought in fruit flies, so new, confused nymphs

wouldn't eat each other, so I could raise them
more gracefully than children.
"Survivors are solitary," the guidebook said,
so I closed it. "They're dispersed by wind."
I'd be lying if I said I wasn't afraid of wind
rasping, dispersing dry leaves. I'm afraid
for myself, for my son, who misses his father,
who does not understand
why things split apart. Last spring,
I showed him the egg case
after nymphs burst out of it
like synapses pulsed loose from our bodies.
It was a knot of fossilized meringue,
re-knitted with no avenue for entry
or exit. I couldn't tell him
how lives fall in and out. I knew almost nothing,

had seen only white, tiny leaps
losing their gathering of colors
to Peperomia's corrugations, to my office's palette
of north light on art prints, books covers.
The nymphs lept so lithely toward the world
I was hard-pressed to deliver them
to someone's garden in time for them to feed,
allowing each its chance
to grow up sated, saved
by the colors of leaf, field, branch, earth,
any colors it needed not to notice
how swiftly it was turning
into itself, how alone.

Before We Parted

All that Spring we walked the dirt road
trying to save things, disguising love
as whatever's threatened—no,
that's not true—we meant to save ourselves.
We brought home praying mantis pods, dug up
mullein, wild azalea, and a plant
I still cannot name; we shredded
the sheer, sagging tents of worm larvae
because we were nosy, greedy.
We needed to believe we were caring
for small, wounded birds
but were watching, in water-filled bottles
and jars, rootlets urging like hairs,
and in the terrarium, for the moment
when mantis cases would burst
from tiny, white lives
needing out, like desires as they begin
to leap through the cells of the brain,
before they start eating each other.

Flordia

A friend tells me how sexual
Florida is, her students in bathing suits,
so languid in their bodies,
so loose and shining
in their desks. Who are their parents,
I wonder; I wish they were mine. The night
she tells me this
I have just left a long marriage.
The heart in my body
cobbles as if over stones,
as if it were made of rectangular
wheels. It needs to go to Florida,
it needs to take a course
in simple lessons: standing,
walking, lying down,
the perspicacious translation
of the outstretched hand.
There are some, it's heard,
you don't have to duck from.

It's in the air there,
my friend says, in the lizards
whose diversity we'd never guess,
the lush flora above which she writes
and watches and dreams us
entire, spumes of hope
and wholeness, wholly in touch, in touch.

Only some of this is true. But I tell you,
my heart is a real, open question...
What if it bounced somewhere other
than arteries, ventricles, veins? Then
you'd have to try to save it.
Listen: do you hear your heart
beating your body together?
Do you hear the magic of body
and spirit uniting?

The Loneliness Bird

My mother has a sparrow in her attic.
She calls us long distance,
saying, "Listen," lifting her receiver
toward the ceiling.
It screeches, chirps. It follows her
to the kitchen, bathroom,
bedroom. It cries
when she's leaving.

I call her neighbor
who crawls through the attic
with a flashlight, looking for spores,
feathers, dung-and-spittle nest,
holes in the rafters. He calls back
to tell me it's her smoke alarm
battery, shorting.

She lifts the trap door,
leaves it seeds, berries, water.
She takes it a folded afghan,

bark strips, leaves. She calls to it
above all her ceilings
and it answers. She's afraid
for its winter, she's afraid
it's dying in the eaves.

On Top of That, the Dog

So: all this will turn to subconscious–whole house
reduced to a closet, an elevator
going down, down, full of tiny rooms
with tinier sofa, chairs, table, bed,
dirty clothes, dishes, trash,
and on top of that, the dog
peeing all over everything, eating your shoes,
your supper. I write this sitting in your house
while you're gone. Your manic-depressive ex-wife
comes in without knocking, asks for more money.
She too will go down when I return
to my unhappy family. I have never understood
the brain's dysfunctions, how it gets crimped,
severed. "I got something to do
up on Coventry," she tells me, but no one ever knows
what. She walks up and down the blocks
every day, talking, singing
to no one. Now she's headed down with you,
whom I'd meant so much to love better.
Your 300-pound grown stepson still sleeps upstairs,
as he does almost always, but he too loses weight,
sinking. Goodbye, almost goodbye, I'm trying so hard to wave
through the layers of memory and regret,
crenellations of love
and grief, darkest valleys of coiled brain
in which we all turn nearly weightless, translucent.

Before the Second Marriage

Here's a chair to sit in
and peruse *The Wall Street Journal,*
futures filling as pork, soybeans, corn

inside the tiny disgestive systems
of thrips. And here's his sofa
with fat roses blown

across the brown ground of its throw,
tendrilous with vines, fringe, ringlets
of perspiration, and the washing machine

he throws almost everything into,
emerging fresh as Joy
or Gain can reconstrue. Here's her soon-to-be

stepdaughter, who never lifts
a finger, his almost-stepson, too good
to be true, her good dog, his rude cat,

their separate bank accounts. Finally,
here's Cheever, whom they'd plotted
to avoid. Soon

they'll begin to shop
for chairs, sofa, table, bed, house,
the furniture and walls of the future,

so unlike those of the past:
rooms in which they shall be utterly
altered in a twinkling,

resurrected in mirrors, refracted
by candlelight. In that heaven
everyone will have equal say

in almost all
but most ordinary matters.

Sad Music

I was not going to tell you
how all night I've lain listening
to men dynamite the frozen Chagrin
because, from this distance, maybe everything sounds
like something else;
the chunks of ice exploding
make soft, barely discernible thuds
like the stereo dropping a record
of lost-love songs in our friend's living roon,
or another friend's foot
dropping onto the floor
the first morning
she doesn't want to live anymore,
or your heart
as my ear lay against it all night
like river pushed and pulled by moon. I was not going to tell
you
how each space between explosions
seems two moments: one saying, *Love,*
the other, *goodbye.* Or perhaps it's that moment
in our friends' lives
between ingnorance
and knowing, that space we'd give almost anything
to go back to,
before anyone hurts.

A little thaw, and water
goes crazy. I know a man and woman
who live by the mouth of the Chagrin:
in March it floods their bedroom,
kitchen, attic. Each year they throw away
everything they have and each April
they start over. I could not do that,
and tonight as I listen
to the river's small, soft convulsions
I'm thinking of the heart's
muffled thunders, detonations. I'm thinking,
as we said, "Life is serious."
I'm thinking how lucky we are

to be on this side
of happy, terrible sin, and of that winter tree
we could not name
in our friend's yard, its branches
creaking upwards
like someone's wishes reaching and curling
to hold something precious
though they were empty.

Chipping Icicles

It would have been so easy, you say,
if only you'd swept them loose
at the beginning! If only you'd paid attention,
taken care of us! Instead, past midnight,
I'd listen so hard
for molecules cracking into ice
on the swell of Lake Erie wave
around the tarsus, rump of a gull, the gill
of a minnow. I wanted to hear air crisping
daily drips from our gutters, splats
from our eaves. So the icicles reach the ground,
spearing crocus bulbs, and all day you lean
with hammer and chisel against the ladder,
smashing rainbows and lights
from our walls. I can see
all the way through our neighbors' house
to the interstate, traffic beyond.
So many cars headed so many places!
But our neighbors sit
at their dining room table, sipping
something. Retired, they must know everything
we don't. I squint to discover
their secret of comfort
and ease, a table, chairs, drinks
toward which a long marriage lurches
where we breathe each other's exhaltations
without anger or blame or remorse. So much
do I need to believe our years lead somewhere
other
than their evidence suggests.

Country Song

When the heat comes to Virginia
there's nothing for it. You can get
a cup of ice and suck.
You can put your head
in the freezer. When the thunderstroms come
the power will go
but you can sit after
on the deck in sopping air
like a wet, wool blanket,
drinking lemony tea. We tell stories
about our great uncles
who owned the ice plants
where the blocks were so heavy
they had to use iron tongs to lift them
onto people's porches. Our parents said, as children,
they ran behind to catch the slivers
which sometimes cut their tongues;
they got their feet all grungy
with horse droppings. Oh what won't we do
for relief from the sweltering? We like the fork lightning
though Papa's third cousin was struck
hugging a tree and all the pennies in his pocket melted.
Some nights it's so bad I'd give anything
for the ice not to melt
just as I would do anything
to take back the pain
our love has caused you.
But it warms in the tea
as rain slides down a windshield
like languid drips from the leaves,
like old tears we haven't cried since childhood
by which light
I write you this poem.

Your Rightful Childhood

We were eleven but Carsie looked sixteen:
bra, garter belt, stockings, lips
that pressed ragged crimson rings on her cigarettes
and shaped circles that rose
high above the schoolyard at recess.

She cursed, and my mother
would not let me go home with her
so I lied. Wedged between two other houses,
her living room was so dim
it was as though they'd walled up the dark;

when she let me in we were blotted.
I thought I'd see her bedroom, but she yelled
Hey old lady, I'm going out.
A woman old enough to be her grandmother
stepped from the kitchen, wiping her hands

on her green apron, asking Carsie when she'd be back:
When you see me.
We walked to Royal's Drugs for her cigarettes,
gum. She loved Elvis
and sang all the words to his songs

the way she said she sang them to her sailor
Friday nights outside St. Helena's Recreation Center.
My mother said her mother
didn't pay attention, never came
to PTA. When her father, who was even older

than her mother, died, Carsie said only
Good riddance. But I listened to her cry
the night the sailor told her
he was going home to marry. A week later
she ran off, we heard, to South Carolina

with a different sailor. I never saw her again.
That night I was supposed to be riding
my bicycle from Linda's. Already my lies
were improving, already I was learning
the paths out of childhood

but not the ones back
as Carsie spat the loose tobacco from her Luckies
and blew smoke toward the uppermost leaves
of the elm. My mother waited for her
to turn up in the paper, Runaway Found Dead

or Pregnant, placed in Florence Crittenden Home.
That was the year the rest of us
started roaming: I'd walk to Jean's,
we'd go to Linda's, then get Diana, Mary Lou
and walk six blocks to Judy's.

We couldn't walk any farther;
there was the river. We walked twenty miles
up and down two miles of sidewalks.
Linda, Mary Lou, and Judy were already swearing
I'm gonna kick my old lady's ass

and some smart-mouthed kid's at school.
The next year they'd join a gang
at the high school, carry knives,
lean against the walls cursing and smoking.
But this year none of us was sure

of the shapes we were taking, those ghosts
down the road the self enters and fills.
We tried to imagine Carsie having children:
it was supposed to hurt.
It was supposed to hurt really bad.

The Fathers

Paul Sieloff clocks out from the Ford plant
and waits for my father to pick him up in his orange truck
but my father's stopped at the liquor store

again. He's devising a story
that keeps him driving in circles;
they'll be late for supper.

All the way home Mr. Sieloff will argue
with himself over whether to tell his wife
to tell my mother. For months,

the answer's been No. Richmond Koonce walks home
from the bank where he's lent several friends
lots of money. In his pinstripe suit,

he opens the door to find crabs
clambering out of the pot, steaming.
He has the nicest life. Saturday

he will hire my father
to replace all his doorknobs, dig
a new cellar. I hate Mr. Koonce

for his beautiful red-haired daughter
who takes ballet, for his ridicule of my fat father,
who weighs more than the other fathers put together,

who sweats as if he were still in Texas.
But my father takes all the kids for rides
in his truck and feeds us ice cream.

Clyde Jennings drives his '49 Chevrolet
six blocks from the drugstore
where he's the pharmacist's assistant,

climbs the stairs to the side entrance
of his angry widowed mother's house
where he lives upstairs with a wife, three children,

two parakeets in three tiny rooms.

He'll stay up half the night
studying for his pharmacology exam

at the kitchen table by a window that pours light
into my sister's and my bedroom.
Only Mr. Mann, the bus driver, leaves for work

at the others come home. He wears a blue uniform
and a wide belt he's put on after strapping his children.
They come out as soon as he's gone

and hide with the rest of us in alleys, bushes.
We're so busy playing we don't know
our fathers are quiet, we don't notice

it's getting dark inside their Chevrolets and Studebakers,
darker still in the basements where they shovel coal
every morning, darkest where they planted us

among the dark millions, and now what is left
but the working out of that, the consequences?
I want Mr. Koonce to die, and Mr. Mann,

never dreaming they'll all be dead
in ten years, except for Mr. Jennings
who'll wander with Alzheimer's, asking everyone

his name, address. My father will lose weight
from many strokes. Mr. Seiloff will die
of a heart attack, Mr. Mann of cerebral hemorrhage.

Mr. Koonce will blow his brains out
to keep from going to jail. But tonight
they're alive, and we're their children

playing outside after dark, not knowing
how we came to live side by side,
Carolyn, Douglas, Janet, Paul, Bobby, Ronnie,

Arelene, Rebecca, Joanne, and Paula,
not even knowing this is our one, only life.
Our fathers come out on our porches to call us in

where lamps splice shadows to theirs.
They look so familiar.
They look like someone we know.

The Mothers

In the far corner where one of the fuchsia
linoleum roses
cracks, the lone cockroach doesn't notice

my face at the kitchen window
where I'm standing with my dead grandmother
on cement blocks, watching the ghost of my young mother

wash dishes. All morning
my grandmother and I have been selling Larkin products
in the rain, taking turns

carrying the satchel, bloated with products—
made beds, spilled milk,
aprons with your favorite meals

stained on them, old dogs and cats, pieces
of Hurricane Hazel, felled trees and the family
huddled in branchly embrace.

Mrs. Koonce, one street over,
needs the most
since the Caterpillars demolished her house.

All that remains
is grass. In her flowered lawn dress
she roams the property

wringing her hands. Her mother is lost
from the corner of their upstairs bedroom
where she sat by lace curtains

blown by summer breeze, tatting. Yes,
we can help her; we have a house
in our memory warehouse—pre-fab,

it comes with DUZ and free Golden Wheat dishes,
a sofa, table, chairs, stairs leading from the coal cellar
to the roof. And here is her husband

alive, mean-spirited, telling my sister and me
to go home; he doesn't want us to play
with his daughter. He hires my father

to dig a shelter under his house
and now all that is left is the shelter.
Next we find Mrs. McPherson

in her brown-shingled 3rd floor apartment,
ironing, plugged into *Queen for a Day*.
Today the woman with rheumatoid arthritis,

nine chldren, no husband, wins the refrigerator
and mink. Mrs. McPherson irons
her husband's collars and cuffs,

all her sprinkled hills and mounds
of laundry. She has just discovered
her daughter is pregnant

by a married man, that her husband's clothes
reek of odd perfume. She keeps ironing.
She is glad to see we have come

and buys boxes of Regrets
and Thank-yous, a bottle
of worn-out migraines, jars of memory

for her mother's Alzheimer's. My grandmother and I
are in a rush; we must tell the mothers
Hurry, the days are eating you alive;

your children and husbands are burning out of themselves,
leaving you alone. We must leave my mother
scouring dried lima beans

and fatback from the pressure cooker;
we must leave her
flicking the kitchen switch at 6 a.m.,

spraying the skittering roaches
with Raid. She knows
it's a losing battle

but why not keep believing
she can win? We're in a hurry.
My grandmother and I keep emptying

our satchel; yet it stays filled.
No one has long. We must go on knocking,
ringing doorbells. There are so many.

Godmother

She lives three houses down from us,
across the street, among musty walls,
25-watt bulbs. Her husband

rocks all day in a corner
in the attic, scribbling his memoirs
with Jack Daniels. He's tired

of her miracles,
absences. He's tired of her
arranging flowers at the church

for baptisms, confirmations.
Each Christmas and birthday
she gives my sister and me

a fresh, embroidered handkerchief
which my mother will not let us use
so we have a collection folded

out of sight for sinuses
and tears. She is the only one
to love us purely.

She asks no questions
about why we are such
a disappointment, so homely,

so mediocre in our studies.
She doesn't care
whether we marry a prince.

Her name is Lee, as in leeward.
She feeds us
graham crackers.

We love her. She keeps
giving us lawn
handkerchiefs. We blow and blow.

Last Date

On July 21, 1958,
the most important place
is the filling station on the corner

of 35th and Granby
where Johnny Hammond and I wait
for the bus to Ocean View

Amusement Park. What is drearier
than an Esso station
on a Saturday afternoon, what is stranger

than the space inside
a thirteen-year-old's heart?
Inside hers

are two gas pumps, a filling station boy
wiping others' windshields,
checking their oil. There's no

unleaded, just Johnny
asking for his ring back,
St. Ignatius with a Celtic cross

stained red. Her heart
is getting crowded. Grow larger,
heart; make room. It's for the best,

this early end
of love: his mother doesn't trust her,
a Protestant, and they could not raise children

on his paper route collections
much less ride to Ocean View, where neither
forsees the wooden roller coaster

demolished. calliope abandoned,
the kewpie dolls and barkers bursting
like lovers, growing up, wandering away.

It's for the best, this dismantling,
this enlarging of hearts. Otherwise
she'd almost always

be pregnant. Otherwise they might grow up
and old together, surrounded
by children, grandchildren, not learning

any other names for Life. They'd never finish
Junior High. They'd be too happy.
They wouldn't know what else to do.

Babysitting

Because I didn't have a boyfriend
I had babies and dirty dishes
and a vacuum cleaner that caught fire
three times as I sucked crumbs, socks,
rushing to make life perfect for the Greggs
before their return. How I hated them

for leaving their children with me,
dirty, hungry, crying
with bath water running, ground beef
bleeding on the counter. How I hated myself
for going back each Saturday night
for thirty-five cents a hour.

They were always laughing
as they left. With her bouncy Dutch-boy hair,
frosted lips, his string tie
and leisure suit, they looked
as if they were dating
instead of charming acquaintances and strangers

into buying Stanley Home Products—
detergent, rug cleaner, mothballs,
vitamins, hair spray, make-up.
This is not about
taking care of children. This is about
locking myself in the bathroom

with products named Stanley.
I let the children almost
kill each other, lie where they fell
groggy, half-in, half-out of bed, and only then
read them a story
about an ugly stepmother, beautiful godmother,

dreams. Hard to imagine them now,
middle-aged, jogging, eating right,
taking good care
with me still inside them, the erasure
in their nightmares, the wish
that never comes true.

Halloween: 1954

On the grate in the living room
my five-year-old cousin Speck from Philadelphia
is kicking my grandfather in the shins.

My grandfather yells until my mother yanks
my cousin away and wakes her brother Frank
who has a headache from driving all this way

so his son can meet his grandfather.
My mother wants my uncle to whip Speck, but
he only asks him to be nice.

My sister's in our darkened bedroom
with a washrag full of ice
and a migraine, though no one calls it that;

she's only eight and my mother says she uses pain
to get attention. It's an hour before supper.
My mother asks my uncle, *Now can we talk?*

They go to the kitchen, where stew simmers,
steams the windows. I'm only ten, but I know
my mother's angry at my uncle, the busy director

of something big in Philadelphia, the one
who predicted my grandfather would come to this
if he married again, the one

who used up all the college money
and never came back until now.
My grandfather has lived with us all year.

He doesn't know our names; he can't be trusted
alone, but almost every night he breaks out
down Dinwiddie and my sister and I

must go find him among the shadows,
shrubbery, alleys. Sometimes he's on someone's porch
rocking and crying. He tells us, *Go away.*

Sometimes we have to give him candy;
then he'll come with us, calling and cursing
names we never heard of. Tonight he rubs

his shins, limps back and forth
between living room and kitchen
while uncle Frank says *he's better off with you*

and my mother says *I can't take any more.*
My sister gets up. My father comes home.
He's been drinking again, but

we don't know it, we're so happy to see him.
At supper he makes us laugh, even uncle Frank
and my mother, my grandfather.   We feel like a family.

Uncle Frank and my father drink beer.
My uncle is happy. In a year he'll be dead
in a taxi, speeding from an airport

with a woman my mother and his wife
have never heard of, but tonight
all he cares about is us:

such attention! He tells us we're pretty,
he tells Speck how wonderful it is
to be with cousins, he cuts holes

in my mother's old sheets.
I'm a ghost.
My sister's a ghost,

and my cousin. I'm so happy
that once we go out in the dark
I do not pinch Speck so hard

or trip him as I'd planned to
as we float up and down the sidewalks with bags,
climbing

to each lit doorway, asking for treats
in exchange for our names, whose house
we've stepped out of, which family.

Christabels

There was this girl, fourteen
when I was fourteen. I'm fifty now,
with emphysema. I've raised two children,
am beyond blood that flushed young eggs.
That August night four girls (my younger sister, I;
her younger sister, she) unlatched screens
of our bedroom windows
while parents slept, my mother turned from my father
in her tricot slip, my father splayed on his back
in boxer shorts, his slack balls plopping
side to side, his snoring covering all sound.

Outside, it was so quiet and dark.
My sister carried the bag of fruit and candy
as we tiptoed through the shush
to meet the girl and her sister midway.
Four together, how we tittered, whispered
while crickets and cicadas and stars crisscrossed
while the place empty for us opened: the curb.

No boys, no money, no blood.
Walk to Where Street.
Take a bus.
Don't talk to sailors.

It's August. I'm up loving girls
before intersections.

I'm up loving you, who must be a little strange
yourself to be reading this poem.

Let's go there together.

Making Up

Is anything else as important?
My neighbor, 15, holds a bag of groceries,
staring from behind the pyracantha
at the couple I've watched all summer,
bronze boy on a bike, blond girl
dancing on her stoop. They've argued,
laughed, hugged and kissed, fought,
the girl with her hands on her hips,
the boy with his fist in the air. They've flown
into each other's arms across the parking lot.

In between I've seen him walking
with my neighbor, their arms
around each other, heading for the pines.

Today the blond practices cheers
for him, his ring back
on her neck chain, tossing August light.
My neighbor stands with frozen dinners
until her mother yells down
they're dripping, spoiling.

Fifteen

To fit in, I lifted "Angel Baby"
from the rack of 45's, slipped it
inside my coat, walked out of the drugstore
with Susan and Irene. Within the week,
my life turned serious: my boyfriend
dumped me, the woman at the drugstore
called Susan's mother, who called Irene's,
agreeing I was too bad
to hang out with. It wasn't fair: I didn't even like the record.
Susan and Irene had drawers jammed with stolen nailpolish,
lipsticks, mascara. They did it all the time;
they did *it* all the time.

Andso I was alone.
And so I smashed the record, threw its shards out,
and promised God *never, if only. . .*

And so I made up a boyfriend
from another town and bought myself
a rhinestone ring from Woolworth's. I swooned
to him half the night on the phone,
I went to his Prom, did it
on the back seat of his Chevrolet.
Soon I would be pregnant, disgraced. My first child
would look just like her father, spend her life
searching for him.

In the girls' room, Susan and Irene
asked me to take off my ring,
let them test it against mirror glass.
It slashed a path across our faces.
It must be real, Susan said to Irene.
It must be real, Irene said to Susan.

The Perfect Life

I don't know how to talk
about my dead, crazy great-aunt Alice
now that the niece who nursed her,
my mother, is far crazier. Shall I begin

with Alice's being wooed
by Uncle Cleve, who sold two of his fish markets
to build her a dream house
with oriental rugs, cedar closets, inside toilet,

a lathed, swirled mahogany bannister?
Or should I begin with the first time
Alice slid down the bannister
backwards, then leap-frogged from end to coffee

table, chewing her hair? No,
that would be too great
a leap, for in between
were joy and dailiness.

We could visit Uncle Cleve's rage and denial
the day the doctor told him no children
was his fault. We could go on their trips
to Chatauqua each summer, sipping mint juleps,

or on his way to Walter Reed, describing
what the loss of an ear does to a face—
my sister and I hiding, terrified.
One day Alice sat on open scissors

left on the damask settee.
After stitches, my mother cut Alice's waist-
length hair with the same scissors. Alice cried;
her hands would not stop twirling and twisting the air

for white waves. My mother bathed her,
packed one satchel, and drove to Eastern State,
where everyone wore white. We couldn't tell one
from another. I want to begin

with the end and end with the beginning,
the place where Aunt Alice, Uncle Cleve,
such good lookers, swing summer evenings
and wave to the envious passersby,

the time before my mother was surprised
by guttings of her memory.
I want to cradle her back
to her honeymoon with the World War II Captain,

my father, as he promises her the moon.

Glamour

My best friend's mother
looked like Rita Hayworth.
After school we'd find her waltzing
to Deep Purple on the monaural with a Pabst
and dust swirlings in a shaft of light,

practicing to leave her fourth husband,
the Master Sergeant she'd left number three for
after the NCO Club dance.
The magic is gone, she said among drags
on Phillip Morrises. I loved most
her mahogany vanity with its three-sided mirror,
covered with henna rinses, lipsticks, creams,
rhinestone earrings like clumps of stars.

My mother said, "Plain people
don't mind aging" to my sister and me,
all bones, braces, and stringy, ash-brown hair.

One day I went over and no one answered.
I looked in the apartment windows
and saw walls
hung with paler rectangles
of nothing
where photographs used to be. I didn't know
where else to go for weeks.

Ella: 1950

Mondays all our backyards were full of laundry,
Tuesdays, our rooms aromatic
with ironing, shirts and dresses

strung across the kitchen.
Each week Ella made magical steam
from Niagara and water, sprinkled the clothes

and rolled them into bolsters,
gave us back pleats, ruffles, collars so beautiful
and hurtful: stiffest cotton cut me,

sanded my neck and underarms.
It was what my mother wanted. For lunch
Ella ate bologna with my mother

in the living room, watching *Love of Life*,
A Secret Storm, *Search for Tomorrow* on the boxy
black-and-white TV. Afternoons the radio was tuned

to *Stella Dallas*, *Ma Perkins*, while Ella
steamed, pressed, folded to the swells
of organ music, the crises

in characters' lives. Some afternoons
someone would call
about my grandfather, who no longer knew

where he lived. Ella would unplug the iron,
walk the streets to find him, listen
to his stories of being betrayed by a witch

the second time around, of living with children
who didn't care about their children
when the house burned to the ground

every night. One Christmas
we found her freezing and fevered
in her heatless house. My mother wrapped her

in blankets, brought her home. I know
I have no business writing this poem.
I was a stupid child; what could I do?

I don't want to remember this.
I want to remember her dancing
away from us with her friends at 3:30

down Dinwiddie toward Liberty Street,
all of them singing, swinging satchels,
laughing and laughing and laughing

over tales within tales within tales.

THREE TRUE STORIES AT THE BACK

Tuberculosis

Early phlegm is yellow,
later, green.
There must be something blue inside the body.
Perhaps infection is blue.
Perhaps gulps of azure sky
cloud the respiratory system
or waft into the skull with songs
of nightingale and melancholy.

Hans Castorp wore his lost beloved's
glass transparency in his chest pocket.
When he caressed it good night
he sought again her essence
as if the soul could be caught,
dried, pinned like a butterfly.
"You have a beautiful catarrh,"
the Directress told him.
Dr. Behrens with his machine
ordered Hans to press his breast against it
"as though it filled you with rapture."

Not everyone comes out well
from treatment, that counterculture
with its own kings and queens,
jacks and princesses. I forgot
what I did for a living
or that I had connections.
Almost out of wind, some of us come to love
the holes and shadows, blood-beads
glistery as jewelry, vacant mists
through which the breeze of a song
might float as if through Keats's lungs
distended in his yard amid dusk's
thin air and eglantine.

Blue Moon

New Year's Eve in detox—
the TV weatherman says a blue moon
will rise, full and dusty.
Toothless Bill, who's been here longest,
says if we wish on this moon on this night
the wish will be granted   out there
where stars collide
and lotteries are decided. Little Helen
names the moon Jesus,
moving from window to window
singing "Jesus on the main line,
tell him what you want"
while Big Helen's shaking worsens.

Poor nurse's aide, pulling a double shift
alone, charged with celebration.
She brings crepe streamers,
brown and purple, measures the tape
to decorate the ceiling, hands out orange balloons
like breatholators, colors of Halloween and Lent.
Sober, we see their tawdriness
but keep twirling and blowing.
Bill's lisped wishes control the ashtray
and remote; his wish comes out "I with"
though he's never been with anyone.

Nonetheless, he leads us in the bunny hop
which, by taking shifts, we hope to keep
kicking until midnight, when we'll run up
and down the halls looking through the windows
for blue light, as if scanning channels,
something nameless each has always wanted
streaming into each room as though lost
as we are, fuller of loneliness and grace,
wanting in even more than we want out.

Down The Road

I'm already there, says my birthday,
though evidently not far enough, say my family
and the doctors. But it's tiring
so I'm taking a break. Where are you, God,
when I need you? Sometimes the people I've needed
have been even needier than I.

One year, my friend and I sat with legs swinging
from the seawall at high tide, toes barely sluicing
the shapes of the waves. Thinking deeply,
my friend declared each of us had already passed
our death-day, that there was a calendar square
waiting, though perhaps already filled
with important appointments, perhaps even the winning
of the Lottery, perhaps even Love or a good fight
or a fine coiffure or *haute couture* on a day
or otherwise flu and laryngitis, writer's block,

each of which would give way
as if they had no lasting power,
as if there were, after all, little sense
in anyone's making plans.

The road is usually still, always the dirt or gravel path
with weedflowers—deadnettle, rue—pushing through.
Tonight my beloved '85 Cadillac is stuck
in a raggedy pothole. One radial tire is flat
but the wire-rim hubcap, coveted enough
by someone one night to have been pried loose with the others
for resale, or prized out of need or love, seems OK.
The road is passing through the rural quiet
with no store, street lamps, or neon, not even a moon.
I'm praying there's a bend past which lies a fork,
one side of which heads straight to town. I'm praying
that all it takes is for me to choose rightly,
I, whose strongest weakness lies in not knowing
how to choose. I've gotten out the map

but cannot see to read it; my fingers race from here
to there, to where. To courage. To getting out of the car
and walking, running, building up breath and muscle.

If only the road hadn't been poured into hills, valleys,
twists, and turns. If only the above weren't a fragment,
like this, like our hope of God and salvation.
If only legs and breath lasted longer. At least the road
keeps going, as if it will outlive us,
as if just by moving we'll soon be somewhere else.
I bank on this as I place one shoe in front of the other.
They're on it. They're getting somewhere.
Let's be sure to meet there;
we've missed each other so.